PYTHON DAY 2
Richard Wagstaff

Copyright © 2014 In A Day Books

All rights reserved.

ISBN: 1499526555

ISBN-13: 978-1499526554

Start Coding Fast

Are you fed up with reading long, boring paragraphs upon paragraphs upon paragraphs of text and just want to get up and running in Python as soon as possible? Well, you're not alone. I hate having to read through masses of text for very little benefit and hence, In A Day Books was born. The goal is simple: Teaching you how to program by cutting the theory and diving straight into 'hands on', practical programming.

Do you have some knowledge of Python and want to learn more? If so, I've got you covered. Here's a list of what you'll learn in Python In A Day 2:

1. CSV's: How to work with CSV files to export data from Python into a Spreadsheet, and vice versa.
2. Web Scraping: How to grab data from Websites using Python.
3. Databases: How to work with a database in Python.
4. GUI's: How to create a Graphical User Interface with Python.

Want to learn a specific topic? Not a problem – you can skip chapters you don't want to learn because different code is used in each chapter. This is also mega helpful if you get hopelessly stuck in a chapter as you can just move on to the next.

If you want a dictionary containing every little bit of Python, this book is not for you. This book has been written for those who want to learn Python fast and want to learn by actually coding programs instead of reading about them. So, are you ready to start coding?

Contents

Part One: CSV Files
1. How To Export Data From Python To A Spreadsheet 3

Part Two: Web Scraping
1. Installation 13
2. Scraping The Web With Python 18

Part Three: Databases
1. Installation 33
2. Using SQL To Talk To Your Database 37
3. Create A User Friendly Database Program 53

Part Four: Graphical User Interface (GUI)
1. Installation 71
2. Making your First Python GUI 75
3. Create An Epic Program That Connects GUI's And Databases 95

Quick References
1. Web Scraping 119
2. Databases 121
3. GUI 123

Welcome!

Word of Caution

If you have a basic knowledge of Python, then this book is for you! If you are a complete beginner, I recommend that you read Python In A Day because this book won't make any sense. Python In A Day can be found on Amazon at the following link:

http://inadaybooks.com/python

Using The Book

The purpose of this section is to let you know the different conventions used in the book.

1. Python 2.7 is used throughout the book. At the time of writing, wxPython does not support a higher version.
2. You can view or download all of the scripts in the book from the In A Day Books website.

   http://www.inadaybooks.com/scripts

3. Code that needs to be added to the script has been formatted like so:

```
Code script example
```
Script number

4. There is some small text in italics beneath the code boxes. This refers to where the script can be found on the website or in the downloaded files.
5. Any output from the script will be formatted like so:

Output formatting

6. Any code that is referenced in the text will be formatted like this `x` and `variableName` are.
7. Backslashes "\" are often used in the book to tell Python to continue where it left off on the next line. So, if there was a long string, you could add a backslash and continue writing the string on the next line. Adding a backslash just makes the code easier to read, especially in the book.

Every example in this book is available on the In A Day Books website. You can view the scripts online or you can download them. Sometimes the code in this book can be difficult to read, so having the scripts will help. The scripts can be found at the following address:

http://www.inadaybooks.com/scripts

CSV's: How To Export Data From Python To A Spreadsheet

"Not only can you not plan the impact you're going to have, you often won't recognize it even while you're having it."
- Dick Costolo, CEO of Twitter

What is a CSV?

CSV is an abbreviation for 'comma separated values'. It stores text in a file like this:

```
Column 1,Column 2,Column 3,Column 4
Value 1,Value 2,Value 3,Value 4
Value 5,Value 6,Value 7,Value 8
```

These CSV files can be opened in spreadsheet program. Whenever a comma is found, the values are separated and the data will appear like so:

Column 1	Column 2	Column 3	Column 4
Value 1	Value 2	Value 3	Value 4
Value 5	Value 6	Value 7	Value 8

Creating the CSV File with Python

We can make CSV files using Python. The first step is to make a new Python file.

*Note: **Do not** name this file csv.py because Python will try to import this file instead of the actual CSV module.*

The CSV file needs to be saved to a directory. For now, we will save it in the same folder as the Python script we're running.

If you are running the script using Terminal or Command Prompt, you can get the path to the script by writing the following:

```
import os
# The path to the script
currentPath = os.path.dirname( \
   os.path.abspath(__file__))
print currentPath
```

csv/script_001.py

If you are running the script using IDLE, you can get the path to the script by writing the following:

```
import os
# The path to the script
currentPath = os.path.dirname( \
  os.path.abspath("__file__"))
print currentPath
```

csv/script_001.py

Note: The only difference is the quotation marks around __file__.

Save the file and run the script. Look at the output and you should see the path to the directory that the script is being run from. Now there's a nifty little trick to keep in your back pocket!

Before we create a CSV file, we need to give it a name. Let's name it 'spreadsheet.csv'. To create the this file, we need to add it to the `currentPath` variable like so:

```
# Make the spreadsheet path
outputCsv = currentPath + '/spreadsheet.csv'
print outputCsv
```

csv/script_002.py

Save the file and run it. Check that the string looks like a proper path to the 'spreadsheet.csv' file.

Reading and Writing Files

File Modes
There are a couple of different modes to handle files in Python.

- **rb** – Reads the file for its contents.
- **wb** – Deletes the current file and enables writing to the file.

If you want to modify files, take a look at the following webpage:

http://inadaybooks.com/filemodes

Writing Files

To open files with these file modes, the `open()` function is used. It takes parameters for the path to the file and the mode. To create the 'spreadsheet.csv' file, we use the writing mode like so:

```
# Open the file
csvFile = open(outputCsv, "wb")
```

csv/script_003.py

Save the file and run it. Take a look in the folder where your script is. You should see a file named 'spreadsheet.csv'. Congratulations! You have just created your first file using a Python script! The file is currently blank though, so let's add some text:

```
# Writing to the file
csvFile.write('Testing')
```

csv/script_004.py

Save the file and run it. If you try opening up the file now, you should see 'Testing' written. Woah, that's awesome! We just wrote a file using Python!

So, whenever you want to write text to files, use this method.

However, this is not really the proper way of writing a CSV file - please excuse me on that one! I wanted to show you quickly how to write text to files.

Writing Data to CSVs

To write CSV files the proper way, we need to create a CSV writer object. The `csv.writer()` function takes the opened CSV file object and a delimiter.

Note: The delimiter is what separates each value. In this case, we will use a comma.

Change:

```
# Writing to the file
csvFile.write('Testing')
```

csv/script_004.py

To:

```
# Create writer object
writer = csv.writer(csvFile, delimiter=',')
```

csv/script_005.py

Save the file and run the script. I got the error 'NameError: name 'csv' is not defined'. Oops, we forgot to import the CSV module. The module is added by changing:

```
import os
```

csv/script_005.py

To:

```
import os, csv
```

csv/script_006.py

Save the file and run it. The output shouldn't contain any errors. If there is an error, it could be that you have named your file 'csv.py'. This makes Python try to import the file it is already running! To fix this, save the file with a new filename and delete the old 'csv.py' file.

Let's actually add some data to the CSV file. Here's some data we can add:

```
# Data to go in csv
row_1 = [1, "Row 1", 123]
row_2 = [2, "Row 2", 456]
row_3 = [3, "Row 3", 789]
```

csv/script_007.py

To write this data to the file, the `.writerow()` function is used like so:

```
# Write rows to csv
writer.writerow(row_1)
writer.writerow(row_2)
writer.writerow(row_3)
```

csv/script_008.py

Save the file and run it.

Go to the folder that contains the CSV file and open it. If you have a spreadsheet program installed, it may ask what the delimiter is. Click on comma and the file should open up for you. When opened, you should be able to see all the data in the spreadsheet program separated into different columns. Cool, huh?

However, if you have massive amounts of data, then using `writer.writerow()` for each row will get very tedious, very quickly. We can use a loop to remove the hard work like so:

```
# All rows
rows = [row_1, row_2, row_3]

# Loop rows and write each
for row in rows:
    writer.writerow(row)
```
csv/script_009.py

This will output exactly the same result, but is much quicker for large amounts of data. Save and run the script to check it works!

Reading CSV Data

We can also extract data from CSV files. This means you can save your spreadsheet as a CSV file and open it up in Python. I recommend creating a new Python file for this section to avoid getting muddled up with writing and reading files.

Note: Once again, do not name the file 'csv.py' otherwise it will try to import itself. This causes many troubles!

Let's get the data out of the 'spreadsheet.csv' file we just created. The first step is getting the path to the file. The following code is very similar to before and the only change is `outputCsv` to `inputCsv`.

```
import os, csv

# The path to the script
currentPath = os.path.dirname( \
  os.path.abspath(__file__))

# Make the spreadsheet path
inputCsv = currentPath + '/spreadsheet.csv'
```
csv/script_010.py

Note: Remember, if you're using IDLE to run the script, add quotation marks around *__file__*.

Now that we have the path, 'spreadsheet.csv' needs to be opened in read mode. The `open()` object is then passed into `csv.reader()` function to create a CSV reader object. This method is similar to writing a CSV file and sounds more complicated than it actually is.

```
# Open file in read mode
csvFile = open(inputCsv, "rb")

# Create reader object
reader = csv.reader(csvFile, delimiter=',')
```
csv/script_011.py

Save the file and run it. There shouldn't be any errors but if there are, fix them before continuing.

To view the data in each row, add the following:

```
# Print out data in file
for row in reader:
    print row
```

Save the file and run the script. You should see each row of the CSV printed out like this:

```
['1', 'Row 1', '123']
```

Wasn't so difficult was it?!

If we want to hold the data in Python, we can create a blank array and then append each row in the loop like this:

```python
# Add data to array
readerData = []
for row in reader:
    readerData.append(row)

print readerData
```

csv/script_013.py

Save the file and run it. All the data should have been added to the `readerData` array and printed out. Very nice work! You can now read CSV files in Python.

Wrapping Up

In this chapter we have learned how to open files in Python and read or write them. I briefly showed you how to write some text to a file and how to get the directory that the script is running from. We wrote some data to a CSV file and then learned how to read data from a CSV file. So now you know how to get data from Python to spreadsheet and vice versa. Good work!

Web Scraping: Installation

"Man is still the most extraordinary computer of all."
- John F Kennedy

What Is Web Scraping?

Web scraping is a method used to extract information from a website. This could include getting the football scores, shopping prices, character details or anything else you see on a web page!

Installation

For Windows

For this chapter, we need to install a Python module called BeautifulSoup. This will help us to extract information from web pages.

To install BeautifulSoup on windows, we are going to use 'pip which allows us to easily download and install Python modules. To install Pip, first we need to install Setuptools and then Pip. Setuptools can be downloaded at the following location:

<http://inadaybooks.com/setuptools>

If you have the 32-bit version of Python (most people), download the file that looks like the following:

setuptools-3.2.win32-py2.7.exe

Note: Setuptools may be a higher version such as 3.3 or 3.4, but make sure you download the Python 2.7 file.

The next step is to download Pip. Go to the following link:

<http://inadaybooks.com/getpip>

Again, you will probably need the win32 version. Don't worry about Pip's version but make sure you select Python 2.7. The filename should look something like the following:

pip-1.5.4.win32-py2.7.exe

When they have both downloaded, go through the Setuptools installation first and then install Pip.

The following steps setup Pip and make it easy for us to use.

Step One

Go to your documents and navigate to where the Python directory was installed. Mine was installed in the following location:

C:\Python27\

Note: If you can't find the folder manually, search for "Python27"!

When you are in the directory, look for the 'Scripts' folder. Open it up and then check that "pip.exe" is in the folder. Now, the beauty of Pip is that we can write the following in the command prompt:

```
> pip install someModule
```

But before we do this, we need to add Pip to the 'path environment variable'. It sounds scarier than it is! Without adding Pip to the path environment variable, we would need to write the following every time we wanted to run Pip:

```
> C:\Python27\Scripts\pip install someModule
```

Step Two

To change the path environment variable, follow the these steps:

1. Right click on "Computer"
2. Click "Properties"
3. Click the "Advanced" tab at the top
4. On the bottom section of the Popup, there is an "Environment Variables" box.
5. Scroll down the Environment Variables box until you find "Path"
6. Click the "Edit" button
7. Add a semi-colon ";" to the end of the path
8. Add "C:\Python27\Scripts" after the semi colon.
9. Click "Ok" to save the changes

Great job on following all of that! To check it works, open up the command prompt in administrator mode.

If you don't know how open command prompt, go to the start

menu and search for "cmd". Right click on "Command Prompt" and then "Run as administrator". When loaded, type the following into the command prompt:

```
> pip install BeautifulSoup4
```

Note: Don't type the '>'. This is just to show that it's a command!

Press Enter to run. If all works well, it will download and install BeautifulSoup for you.

There were plenty of steps here, but you have Pip now! Pip is a massive hassle to set up, but it does make adding modules a dream.

For Mac & Linux

For this chapter, we need to install a module called BeautifulSoup. To do this, we are going to use 'Pip' which allows us to easily download and install Python modules.

The first step is to open up the Terminal. Terminal is found in Applications - Utilities on the Mac. For Linux, I recommend searching for Terminal as its location may vary depending on the distribution.

When the Terminal is open, write the commands below.

Note: I have made them available on the In A Day Books website so you don't have to write them out.

```
$ wget http://inadaybooks.com/pip-1.5.2.tar.gz
$ tar xzf pip-1.5.2.tar.gz
$ cd pip-1.5.2
$ python setup.py install
```

And that's it!

Now we can install BeautifulSoup by running:

```
$ pip install BeautifulSoup4
```

Scraping The Web With Python

"The Web as I envisaged it, we have not seen it yet. The future is still so much bigger than the past."
- Tim Berners-Lee, Inventor of the World Wide Web

To scrape a website in Python, we need to extract data from the source code. Website source code is written in HTML, so some basic knowledge would be helpful. To take a look at some website source code, go to your web browser and look for something like 'View Source' or 'Page Source'. It's usually found in the Tools menu. When you find it, click it and the HTML source code for that page will be shown.

Note: You can complete the chapter without a basic understanding of HTML, but some knowledge is helpful.

We need a website with some data to scrape. I made a website specifically for this chapter and can be found here:

http://inadaybooks.com/justiceleague

The website contains information about The Justice League and has character profiles for the members. The target is to use Python to extract the list of The Justice League members from the website.

Step One: Access the HTML

The urllib2 Module

To get the website source code, we can use the `urllib2` module. Create a new file and import the module like so:

```
import urllib2
```
Web scraping/script_001.py

Save the file and run it. Make sure there are no errors.

To get the source code of the web page, the `urllib2.urlopen()` function is used like so:

```
# Open webpage
webpage = urllib2.urlopen( \
  "http://inadaybooks.com/justiceleague")

print webpage
```
Web scraping/script_002.py

Save the file and run the script. Hmm, the output prints out some kind of object, which does not look much like website source code!

Enter BeautifulSoup

The BeautifulSoup module can read these objects for us. To use BeautifulSoup, add the following:

```
from bs4 import BeautifulSoup
```
Web scraping/script_003.py

Note: Make sure you import BeautifulSoup at the top of the script.

Now we can print out the source code of the `webpage` object by changing:

```
print webpage
```

Web scraping/script_002.py

To:

```
print BeautifulSoup(webpage)
```

Web scraping/script_003.py

Save the file and run the script. The output will return lots of lines of HTML code. Yay! This is exactly what we wanted.

Playing with Soup

BeautifulSoup has a couple of neat shortcuts. For example, we can get the title of the webpage using the `.title` function like so:

```
# Convert to BeautifulSoup
soup = BeautifulSoup(webpage)
print soup.title
```

Web scraping/script_004.py

Save the file and run it. And boom, in a couple of lines we have retrieved the title of the website. To get the content inside the body tag, we can use the following:

```
print soup.body
```

Web scraping/script_005.py

Save the file and run it. Just the code in the body of the website should be printed out.

That's your taster! There are plenty more tricks, so look out for them later in the chapter.

Step Two: Extract the Names of The Justice League Members

To extract the names, we need to figure out where they are in the HTML code. I'll run through how I do this.

I use 'Developer Tools' in the Google Chrome browser. It allows me to click through sections of the code and figure out quickly where the members are located. Here's a screenshot of how it looks:

```
Q | Elements  Network  Sources  Timeline  Profiles  Resources  Audits  Con
   <!DOCTYPE html>
  ▼<html>
    ▶ <head>...</head>
    ▼ <body>
      ▼ <div id="container">
        ▶ <div class="block">...</div>
        ▶ <div class="block">...</div>
        ▶ <div class="block">...</div>
        ▼ <div class="block">
            <h2>Information</h2>
          ▶ <div class="separator">...</div>
          ▶ <div class="separator">...</div>
          ▶ <div class="separator">...</div>
          ▼ <div class="separator">
              <div class="info_left">Members</div>
            ▼ <div class="info_right">
              ▼ <p>
                  <a href="people/aquaman.html" title="Aquaman">Aquamar
                </p>
              ▶ <p>...</p>
              ▶ <p>...</p>
```

So, the members can be found by using the following steps:

1. `<div id="container">`
2. The fourth `<div class="block">`
3. The fourth `<div class="separator">`

4. `<div class="info_right">`

The member names are stored in the "info_right" `div`. Try looking at developer tools or your browser's alternative and getting to the member location by yourself.

Note: This example website is very simple, and 'real world' websites will probably be more complicated to figure out. It takes a bit of practice before you get the knack of looking through website code.

Let's follow the list from above and extract the member names from the source code.

1. Get <div id="container">
BeautifulSoup allows us to search for `div`'s by attributes such as class, id and style. To get the contents of `<div id="container">`, we can use the `.find()` function like so:

```
# Get the contents container div
divContainer = soup.find("div", {"id":"container"})
print divContainer
```

Web scraping/script_006.py

Save the file and run it. The output will print out the content inside the container `div`.

2. Get the fourth <div class="block">
For this, we will use the `.findAll()` function. The difference is that `.findAll()` will return every `div` that matches the search, instead of the first time the div appears.

This time, we are going to search inside `divContainer()` instead of the entire source code. Add the following just beneath the `divContainer` object:

```
divBlock = divContainer.findAll("div", \
   {"class":"block"})
print divBlock
```

Web scraping/script_007.py

Save the file and run the script. Take a close look at the output - each of the `div`'s with the class "block" have been added to an array. The `div` we want is number four, which we can get by using:

```
print divBlock[3]
```

Web scraping/script_008.py

Note: Remember that Python starts counting from zero, so the fourth element in the array is found by searching for [3]. Blame computer scientists!

Save the file and run it. The massive array should be gone, leaving us with the `div` that contains the characters. We are getting there!

3. Get the fourth <div class="separator">

We need to search within the fourth `divBlock` to get all the `div`'s with the class "separator". This is done like so:

```
divSep = divBlock[3].findAll("div", \
   {"class":"separator"})
print divSep
```

Web scraping/script_009.py

Save the file and run it. An array will be outputted. We need the forth `div` in the array and can be found like so:

```
print divSep[3]
```
Web scraping/script_010.py

Save the file and run it. Take a look at the output. Okay, this is good. The members have been isolated so we can now extract their names.

4. Extracting Member Names

Take a moment to have a think about how you could get the names of the members out of the code.

Hint: We need to search for something again!

In my opinion, we don't need to search for the `<div class="info_right">` because the member names are the only elements to have `a` tags in this section of the code. We can use `.findAll()` for the `a` tags like so:

```
members = divSep[3].findAll("a")
print members
```
Web scraping/script_011.py

Save the file and run it. The output should show an array of all the `a` tags. Result! Now we are getting somewhere.

To get rid of those pesky `a` tags, we can use the `.get_text()` function from the BeautifulSoup module. So, let's loop through the `members` array and print out each name like so:

```
# Loop through members
for member in members:
    # Strip <a> tags
    print member.get_text()
```
Web scraping/script_012.py

Save the file and run it. Big smiles! All of the names are printed out without a tags. Now that is pretty cool.

Playing With The 'a' Tags

To get the title attribute from the a tag, we can use the `.get()` function.

Change:

```
print member.get_text()
```

Web scraping/script_012.py

To:

```
print member.get("title")
```

Web scraping/script_013.py

Note: The `.get()` function looks through the member variable and extracts the value of "title".

Save the file and run it. The title attributes for each link will be printed out.

BeautifulSoup can get any attribute inside any tag. This means we can get the href of the a tag by swapping "title" for "href" like so:

```
print member.get("href")
```

Web scraping/script_014.py

Save the file and run it. You should see the href's printed out.

Well, that brings us to the end of this section. We have successfully extracted the member names from the website using Python.

Step Three: Web Crawling

Now that we have the href strings, we can add them to the original URL and open the web pages for each of the members. We can then scrape the data we want from each of these web pages. Now that is pretty awesome.

Fun fact: This is basically how a web crawler works and is how Google indexes pages on a website.

Open up the Justice League website and click on one of the members. The member page contains information such as real name, alias and alignment. Let's extract this data for each member using Python.

Actually Web Crawling

In the `for` loop we created earlier, we need to add the href strings to the original URL and open up the web page. Here's the code:

```
for member in members:
    # Strip <a> tags
    href = member.get("href")
    # Create url to open
    url = "http://inadaybooks.com/justiceleague"+href
    # Open url
    mPage = urllib2.urlopen(url)
```

Web scraping/script_015.py

Save the file and run it. It may take a little while to run because it is opening up the webpages for each member. If no errors are returned, then we are good to go!

To keep the `for` loop relatively clean, we can send the web page object to a function and extract the data there. The name of the function will be extractMData() and will take the parameter webpage like so:

```
def extractMData(webpage):
    soup = BeautifulSoup(webpage)
    print soup.title
```
Web scraping/script_016.py

And then call the extractMData() function by adding the following to the for loop:

```
extractMData(mPage)
```
Web scraping/script_016.py

Save the file and run the script. If you get an error, check that the function is defined before the for loop.

If everything worked properly, the titles for each web page will be printed out.

Locating Character Details
Using developer tools or otherwise, we need to figure out how to get the data. Take a look at the following screenshot of the code for the member page:

```
Q | Elements  Network  Sources  Timeline  Profiles  Resources  Audits
  <!DOCTYPE html>
▼ <html>
  ▶ <head>…</head>
  ▼ <body>
     ▼ <div id="container">
        ▶ <div class="block">…</div>
        ▶ <div class="block">…</div>
        ▶ <div class="block">…</div>
        ▼ <div class="block">
           <h2>Information</h2>
           ▼ <div class="separator">
              <div class="info_left">Real Name</div>
              <div class="info_right">Arthur Curry</div>
             </div>
           ▼ <div class="separator">
              <div class="info_left">Alias</div>
              <div class="info_right">Aquaman</div>
             </div>
           ▶ <div class="separator">…</div>
```

From the image above, we can get to the character's information using the following steps:

1. The fourth `<div class="block">`
2. Character details are found in each `<div class="separator">`

I can see two ways that we can extract the data:

1. Get the fourth `<div class="block">` and then get each `<div class="separator">`. Then we could loop through each "separator" div and print out the text in the "info_left" and the "info_right" `div`'s.
2. Get the fourth `<div class="block">`. Then find all of the `div`'s that have the class "info_left" and "info_right". We can then make a loop and print out the text from both arrays.

I am going to go with the second option. It looks like it will be quicker because there is one less step to get the data. Well, that's the plan anyway!

Extracting the Data

Step 1 - Get the fourth <div class="block">
To get the fourth <div class="block">, we can use the .findAll() function. Add the following to the extractMData() function:

```
# Find all the divs with class block
divBlock = divContainer.findAll("div", \
    {"class":"block"})
print divBlock[3]
```

Web scraping/script_017.py

Save the file and run the script. The information should be printed out for each character.

Step 2 – Get "info_left" and "info_right"
We can use .findAll() to search for div's with the "info_left" and "info_right" classes.

```
info = divBlock[3]

# Extract info_left and info_right divs
getLeft = info.findAll("div", {"class":"info_left"})
getRight = info.findAll("div",{"class":"info_right"})

print getLeft
print getRight
```

Web scraping/script_018.py

Save the file and run it. The output should look something

like the following:

```
[<div class="info_left">Real Name</div>, <div
class="info_left">Alias</div>, <div
class="info_left">Alignment</div>, <div
class="info_left">Gender</div>, <div
class="info_left">Height</div>]

[<div class="info_right">Zatanna Zatara</div>, <div
class="info_right">Zatanna</div>, <div
class="info_right">Good</div>, <div
class="info_right">Female</div>, <div
class="info_right">Unknown</div>]
```

Output from script_018.py

As you can see, two arrays for each character should be printed out. The first array contains the type of information, and the other contains the values.

Prettifying the Data

At the moment, the output is not very easy to read. We could get rid of the tags and prettify the data so it looks something like this:

Real Name: Bruce Wayne
Alias: Batman
Alignment: Good
Gender: Male
Height: 6ft 2in

To do this, we can make a loop that counts from zero to the length of the `getLeft` array. Then we can extract the data for the `getLeft` and `getRight` arrays and then put it all together in a pretty format. Here's the code:

```
for i in range(0,len(getLeft)):
    textLeft = getLeft[i].get_text()
    textRight = getRight[i].get_text()
    print textLeft + ": " + textRight
```

Web scraping/script_019.py

Save the file and run it.

Wow! That definitely looks better but it is still a lot to take in. If we are being really fussy, we could add a break after each character. Add the following outside the `for` loop we have just created:

```
print ""
```

Web scraping/script_020.py

Save the file and run it. If you put the break in the correct place, the data will be separated for each character, making the output so much easier to read.

Wrapping Up

We have learned how to use urllib2 and BeautifulSoup to scrape a website. The urllib2 module opens up webpages which we can view using BeautifulSoup. BeautifulSoup allows us pick our way through the code to find `div`'s, tables, and other HTML tags. It also allows us to search for tags with a certain style, class, id or other. We scraped a web page to extract the names of The Justice League members and then opened up each of the member's own pages to extract specific information. Basically, we created a little web crawler!

BONUS! I have created a chapter extra where I show you how to:

1. Create a progress bar for the script
2. Export the member data to a CSV file

Sounds good? You can sign up and download it from here:

http://www.inadaybooks.com/scripts/

Databases: Installation

"Most good programmers do programming not because they expect to get paid or get adulation by the public, but because it is fun to program."
- Linus Tovalds, Linux

What is a Database?

A database is a collection of data. They allow us to store large amounts of data and retrieve it very quickly.

The database system we are using in this book is called SQLite. SQLite is perfect to get started in databases because it does not require any complicated setup.

Installation

For Windows
To download SQLite, go to the following webpage:

http://inadaybooks.com/sqlite

Find the header 'Precompiled Binaries for Windows'. Now look for the "sqlite-shell" file and download it. The file should look something like the following:

> sqlite-shell-win32-x86-3080200.zip

Note: The number on the end is the version number, and may be different.

Find the file in your documents. Right click on the file and then select "Extract all" and then When the file has unzipped, a folder will be created that contains a file called "sqlite3.exe".

Now, click on "Computer" and then click on "Local Disk (C:)". Create a new folder here, name it "sqlite" and move the "sqlite3.exe" file into this folder.

Go back to the SQLite download page and download the "sqlite-dll" file. It looks something like:

> sqlite-dll-win32-x86-3080200.zip

When the file is downloaded, unzip it. Copy and paste everything from inside the unzipped folder into the sqlite folder that you just created.

Just like for Pip in the web scraping chapter, we can edit the path environment variable to include SQLite. Here are the instructions:

1. Right click on "**Computer**"
2. Click "**Properties**"
3. Click the "**Advanced**" tab at the top
4. On the bottom section of the Popup, there is an

"**Environment Variables**" box.

5. Scroll down the Environment Variables box until you find "**Path**"
6. Click the "**Edit**" button
7. Add a semi-colon ";" to the end of the path
8. Add "**C:\sqlite**" after the semi colon.
9. Click "**Ok**" to save the changes

Let's check everything works by doing the following:

1. Open up the command prompt by searching for "**cmd**" in the start menu.
2. Type in "**sqlite3**" and press enter.
3. If no errors are shown, then SQLite3 was installed correctly.

For Mac

Great news! SQLite3 comes preinstalled with Mac, so you don't need to do anything! If you want to check that SQLite3 is installed, open up the Terminal by going to Applications - Utilities - Terminal. Then enter the following command:

```
$ sqlite3
```

Something like the following should be returned:

```
SQLite version 3.7.12 2012-04-03 19:43:07
Enter ".help" for instructions
Enter SQL statements terminated with a ";"
```

For Linux

You may have SQLite3 already installed if you are using Linux. To check, open up the Terminal. The easiest way to do this is to search for "Terminal" and then click on the icon. Now write the following command:

```
$ sqlite3
```

You should see something like the following output:

```
SQLite version 3.7.13 2012-06-11 02:05:22
Enter ".help" for instructions
Enter SQL statements terminated with a ";"
```

If you get an error, then SQLite3 isn't installed. To install it, run the following command:

```
$ sudo apt-get install sqlite3
```

Note: I have made these commands available on the In A Day Books website so that you don't have to type it all in.

SQL: Talking To Your Database
"Details matter, it's worth waiting to get it right."
- Steve Jobs, Co-Founder of Apple

Getting Started

In this chapter, we are going to learn some SQL and how to make it work with Python. As this is a Python book, I will only show you some SQL basics and won't go into too much detail.

To use SQLite 3 in Python, we need to import the module by using `import sqlite3`. We can then create a database using the `.connect()` function from SQLite 3 module like so:

```
import sqlite3

# Connect to database 'simpsons.db'
conn = sqlite3.connect('simpsons.db')
```
Databases/script_001.py

If the database in `.connect()` does not already exist, then SQLite will create it for us. Nifty, huh?

Save the file and run the script. If there are no errors, then you have successfully created your very first database using Python.

Adding a Table to the Database

About Tables
A database can contain many different tables. For example, there could be a table that contains information about the characters in The Simpsons. There could also be another table for the buildings in Springfield, such as the Elementary School and Nuclear Power Plant. The information for both would be held in one database, but in different tables.

Creating a Table
Let's create a table that contains the following information about the characters in The Simpsons:

1. Name
2. Gender
3. Age
4. Occupation

The table will be named "SIMPSON_INFO". To create this table, we need to use the following SQL code:

```
CREATE TABLE SIMPSON_INFO (
ID INT PRIMARY KEY,
NAME TEXT,
GENDER TEXT,
AGE INT,
OCCUPATION TEXT );
```

Example SQL Code

Here's a breakdown of the SQL code:

Line 1
- Starts the creation of the `SIMPSON_INFO` table.

Line 2
- Creates a column in the table named `ID`.
- The `INT` part tells the database to only allow integer values in the column.
- The `PRIMARY KEY` sets the rule so that each value in the column is unique. It will not allow any value to appear twice. So '1' or '2' or '1572' cannot appear twice in this column.
- The `AUTOINCREMENT` part is used so that the database automatically creates a new, incremented ID for us. For example, if the ID on the previous row was '3', the value for ID on the next row would be automatically set to '4'.

Note: This is by far the most complicated line. Try not to worry about it, you can always look this up when you are creating a new table.

Line 3
- Creates a column named `NAME`.
- The `TEXT` part tells the database to only allow text values in this column.

Line 4
- Creates a column named `GENDER`.
- The `TEXT` part tells the database to only allow text

values in this column.

Line 5
- Creates a column named AGE.
- The INT part tells the database to only allow integer values in this column.

Line 6
- Creates a column named OCCUPATION.
- The TEXT part tells the database to only allow text values in this column.

Note: Be careful not to include a comma on the last line of your SQL. SQL really, really doesn't like the comma and will return an error.

Here's what the SIMPSON_INFO table will look like:

ID	Name	Gender	Age	Occupation
Integer Values	Text Values	Text Values	Integer Values	Text Values

So, we need to run the SQL code in the Python program. To do this, we can place a string of SQL code inside a function called .execute(). To create the table, the code looks like this:

```
# Create table named SIMPSON_INFO
conn.execute("CREATE TABLE SIMPSON_INFO( \
    ID INTEGERPRIMARY KEY AUTOINCREMENT, \
    NAME TEXT, \
    GENDER TEXT, \
    AGE INT, \
```

```
    OCCUPATION TEXT \
);")
```

Databases/script_002.py

Note: The backslash "\" tells Python to continue where it left off on the next line. This makes the code more readable, especially in the book. You don't need to include the backslashes, but make sure you write the entire string on one line.

Save the file and run the script. If no errors are returned, we will assume that the table was created successfully. Don't worry – we will start getting some confirmation from the program soon!

More Column Types
There are three other types of columns:

REAL
- Stores numbers with a decimal point. For example, 1.2 or 1.4523.

NUMERIC
- Converts whatever is inputted into an integer or real number. This includes text. And yes, text can be converted to a number!

NONE
- Holds any type of value.

Inserting Data into the Database

SQL To Add a Row
We need to know some SQL code that inserts data into the

database. To add Bart Simpson to the SIMPSON_INFO table, the SQL code looks like this:

```
INSERT INTO SIMPSON_INFO (NAME, GENDER, AGE,
OCCUPATION) VALUES ('Bart Simpson', 'Male', 10,
'Student')
```
Example SQL Code

The first pair of brackets contains the column names that we want to add data to. The second pair of brackets contains the data to insert for each column name.

Note: You may be wondering where the ID column is. SQLite automatically adds this for us because we used primary key and autoincrement when we set up the table.

Here's what the table will look like when the SQL is run.

ID	Name	Gender	Age	Occupation
1	Bart Simpson	Male	10	Student

The column names and values don't have to be organised in the same order as the table. For example, we could also write:

```
INSERT INTO SIMPSON_INFO (GENDER, AGE, OCCUPATION,
NAME) VALUES ('Male', 10, 'Student', 'Bart Simpson')
```
Example SQL Code

Adding Your First Row with Python

To add a character to the table, we need to place the SQL code in the `.execute()` function just like before. Add the following to the script:

```python
# Add Bart Simpson to table
conn.execute("INSERT INTO SIMPSON_INFO \
    (NAME, GENDER, AGE, OCCUPATION) VALUES \
    ('Bart Simpson', 'Male', 10, 'Student')");
```

Databases/script_003.py

Whenever we make any changes to the database, we need to save them by using the `.commit()` function like so:

```python
# Save changes
conn.commit()
```

Databases/script_003.py

Save the file and run the script. If you did the same as me, you will get an error that reads:

`OperationalError: table SIMPSON_INFO already exists`

Oops! To fix this error, we need to remove the code that creates the `SIMPSON_INFO` table as the script was trying to create a table that already exists. When removed, we should be left with the following:

```python
import sqlite3

# Connect to database 'simpsons.db'
conn= sqlite3.connect('simpsons.db')

# Add Bart Simpson to table
conn.execute("INSERT INTO SIMPSON_INFO \
    (NAME, GENDER, AGE, OCCUPATION) VALUES \
```

```
    ('Bart Simpson', 'Male', 10, 'Student')");
```

```
# Save changes
conn.commit()
```

Databases/script_004.py

Save the file and run it again. You should see no errors, yay!

But, how to we know that the character was added successfully? Allow me to introduce the `.total_changes` function. As you may have guessed, it tells us the number of changes that have been made to the database. Add the following just below the `.commit()` line:

```
# Print number of changes to database
changes=conn.total_changes
print"Number of changes:", changes
```

Databases/script_005.py

Save the file and run the script. You should see that one change was made. Result!

Let's add Lisa and Homer Simpson to the `SIMPSON_INFO` table. Change the following:

```
# Add Bart Simpson to table
conn.execute("INSERT INTO SIMPSON_INFO \
    (NAME, GENDER, AGE, OCCUPATION) VALUES \
    ('Bart Simpson', 'Male', 10, 'Student')");
```

Databases/script_005.py

To:

```python
# Add Homer Simpson to table
conn.execute("INSERT INTO SIMPSON_INFO \
    (NAME, GENDER, AGE, OCCUPATION) VALUES \
    ('Homer Simpson', 'Male', 40, 'Nuclear Plant')");

# Add Lisa Simpson to table
conn.execute("INSERT INTO SIMPSON_INFO \
    (NAME, GENDER, AGE, OCCUPATION) VALUES \
    ('Lisa Simpson', 'Female', 8, 'Student')");
```
Databases/script_006.py

Save the file and run it. The output should say that two changes were made to the database.

Extracting Data from the Database

SQL for Viewing Data

It would be cool if we could actually see the information in the table. Well, here's the magical SQL code we need:

```sql
SELECT ID, NAME, GENDER, AGE, OCCUPATION from SIMPSON_INFO
```
Example SQL Code

That's not so difficult is it?! This code gets all the rows of data for the selected columns. As before, we need to place the SQL into the `.execute()` function and then print out the results. Modify your script and make it look like this:

```python
import sqlite3

# Connect to database 'simpsons.db'
conn= sqlite3.connect('simpsons.db')

# Get data from database
cursor = conn.execute("SELECT ID, NAME,\
    GENDER, AGE, OCCUPATION from SIMPSON_INFO")
print cursor
```

Databases/script_007.py

Note: Cursor is a term often used for handling the database.

Save the file and run it. Hmm, this is what was printed out for me:

`<sqlite3.Cursor object at 0x103b59c70>`

That doesn't look much like our data. However, we can extract the data from this object using the `.fetchall()` function like so:

```
# Get data from cursor
rows = cursor.fetchall()
print rows
```
Databases/script_008.py

Save the file and run it. Take a look at the output. Each row should be returned in it's own array like so:

`(1, u'Bart Simpson', u'Male', 10, u'Student')`

And there's our data!

The text values look a bit strange. Don't worry about them though. The `u' '` means they are formatted in Unicode and it is fine to leave them as they are.

SQL Shortcut

Hold onto your hats, you are going to love this shortcut! To select all of the columns, use * instead of each column name. So, modify the following:

```
cursor = conn.execute("SELECT \
  ID, NAME, GENDER, AGE, OCCUPATION \
  from SIMPSON_INFO")
```

Databases/script_008.py

To:

```
cursor = conn.execute("SELECT * from SIMPSON_INFO")
```

Databases/script_009.py

Save the file and run it. The output should be exactly the same. Less effort for the same result equals a good win!

Viewing Specific Data

What if we only want data for a certain character, just the females or people with a particular job? To do this, we can add "where" onto the end of the SELECT SQL code followed by the column name and the data we want to search for. Here are some examples:

```
SELECT * from SIMPSON_INFO where NAME='Homer Simpson'
SELECT * from SIMPSON_INFO where GENDER='Female'
SELECT * from SIMPSON_INFO where OCCUPATION='Student'
```

Databases/script_010.py

Try out the above SQL code see the outputs. If you get stuck, the full script can be found on the In A Day Books website.

Note: The value is case sensitive.

Deleting Data from the Database

Deleting a Specific Row

If you followed everything I have done previously, you may have noticed that there are two Bart Simpson entries in the table. If you do not have duplicate Bart Simpson entries, choose a character to delete and make a note of the ID. The SQL code to delete the row with ID = 2 is:

```
DELETE from SIMPSON_INFO where ID=2
```

Example SQL Code

That code is almost English! Anyway, this will delete every row in "SIMPSON_INFO" has an ID = 2. Here is the full code – the only new part is the 'delete' SQL on line 7:

```python
import sqlite3

# Connect to database 'simpsons.db'
conn = sqlite3.connect('simpsons.db')

# Delete rows with ID=2
conn.execute("DELETE from SIMPSON_INFO where ID=2")

# Save changes
conn.commit()

# Print number of changes
changes = conn.total_changes
print "Number of changes: ",changes

# Get data from database
```

```
cursor = conn.execute("SELECT * from SIMPSON_INFO")

# Extract data from cursor
rows = cursor.fetchall()
print rows
```
Databases/script_011.py

Save the file and run it. The output should show that the entry no longer exists in the table.

Delete Based on Other Values
We can delete rows based on character names, gender or any other column value like so:

```
DELETE from SIMPSON_INFO where NAME='Bart Simpson'
```
Example SQL Code

In this case, the SQL would delete every row where the value in the NAME column is equal to "Bart Simpson".

Updating Data in the Database

SQL to Update Information
What if there was a birthday, a spelling mistake or a character changed their job? Well, we could delete them and then add a new row with the updated information. This is a bit messy though, so we will use the UPDATE functionality in SQL. Here is the SQL statement that changes Homer Simpson's age to 41:

```
UPDATE SIMPSON_INFO set AGE=41 where NAME='Homer Simpson'
```
Example SQL Code

So, to update Homer Simpson, change:

```
# Delete rows with ID=2
conn.execute("DELETE from SIMPSON_INFO \
where ID=2")
```

Databases/script_011.py

To:

```
# Make Homer Simpsons age 41
conn.execute("UPDATE SIMPSON_INFO \
set AGE=41 where NAME='Homer Simpson'")
```

Databases/script_012.py

Save the file and run it. Check the number of changes and that Homer Simpson's age has been changed to 41. Ah, perfect!

Delete a Table in the Database

Deleting a table is pretty easy. Here's the SQL:

```
DROP TABLE table_name
```

Example SQL Code

Add the following code just before the cursor variable:

```
# Delete the table
conn.execute("DROP TABLE SIMPSON_INFO")
```

Databases/script_013.py

Save the file and run it. You should see an error saying that there is no such table called `SIMPSON_INFO`. Result! The table has been deleted.

Wrapping Up

Phew. That was a pretty hefty chapter! We have covered a range of SQL commands including creating databases, tables, inserting data, updating data and more. I have shown you some commands here, but if you ever get stuck then I advise you to use Google or learn SQL. We will be using what we've learned here to build a Python program to handle databases in the next chapter.

Create A User Friendly Database Program

"People always fear change. People feared electricity when it was invented, didn't they? People feared coal, they feared gas-powered engines... There will always be ignorance, and ignorance leads to fear. But with time, people will come to accept their silicon masters."

- Bill Gates, Co-founder of Microsoft

Introduction

In this chapter we are going to make a program that allows us to do the following:

1. Create a new table
2. Add new characters
3. View all character details
4. View specific character details
5. Delete a character

Step One: Create the Table

The first step is to create a new Python script and then make a function that adds the `SIMPSON_INFO` table to the database.

```python
import sqlite3

# Connect to simpsons database
conn = sqlite3.connect('simpsons.db')

def createTable():
    conn.execute("CREATE TABLE SIMPSON_INFO( \
        ID INTEGER PRIMARY KEY AUTOINCREMENT, \
        NAME TEXT, \
        GENDER TEXT, \
        AGE INT, \
        OCCUPATION TEXT \
        );")

createTable()
```

Database Program/script_001.py

Save the file and run the script. There shouldn't be any errors.

Can you remember in the previous chapter when we left the "create table" code in the script? We got an error saying that the table already exists. Well, we can fix that by changing the SQL code to check if the table exists before trying to create it. Change:

```
CREATE TABLE SIMPSON_INFO
```
Database Program/script_001.py

To:

```
CREATE TABLE if not exists SIMPSON_INFO
```
Database Program/script_002.py

Save the file and run the script. You should see that no errors are returned.

Step Two: Adding Characters to the Database

User Inputs

Let's create a function that allows the user to add characters to the database. The function will ask the user to input the the name, gender, age and occupation of the character like so:

```python
def newCharacter():
    print '\nAdding a new character...'

    # Take inputs
    name = raw_input('Name: ')
    gender = raw_input('Gender: ')
    age = raw_input('Age: ')
    occupation = raw_input('Occupation: ')
```
Database Program/script_003.py

Then we need to call the function:

```python
newCharacter()
```
Database Program/script_003.py

Save the file and run it. It should ask you to input the name, gender, age and occupation. Enter some values and check the script runs through without any errors.

SQL To Add A Character

We need to take these inputs and create an SQL statement from them to add a character. As a reference, here's what the SQL code needs to look like:

```
INSERT INTO SIMPSON_INFO (NAME, GENDER, AGE, OCCUPATION) VALUES ('Bart Simpson', 'Male', 10, 'Student')
```

The user inputs need to be placed in the `VALUES` part of the SQL. So, we need to create a string from the inputs that looks like the following:

```
'Bart Simpson', 'Male', 10, 'Student'
```
Reference String

Cool Stuff: Inserting Variables Into Strings
The `.format()` function inserts variables into strings by looking for `{}` in the string and replacing it with a value. Here are a couple of examples to try:

```python
print 'Epic number: {}!'.format(2)
print 'Also strings: {}!'.format("Hello")
print 'First: {}, Second: {}'.format(1, 2)
```

It's a pretty nice little trick.

Back To SQL
To make the values part of the SQL command, we can use the `.format()` function. Add the following to the `newCharacter()` function:

```python
# Create values part of sql command
val_str = "'{}', '{}', {}, '{}'".format(\
    name, gender, age, occupation)
print val_str
```
Database Program/script_004.py

Save the file and run it. Go through the user inputs and then Python should print out a string using the values you entered. Here's the SQL reference again - check that all of your quotes and commas are in the correct place:

```
'Bart Simpson', 'Male', 10, 'Student'
```
Reference String

The next step is to add `val_str` to the rest of the SQL string. We can use the `.format()` function again like so:

```
sql_str = "INSERT INTO SIMPSON_INFO \
    (NAME, GENDER, AGE, OCCUPATION) \
    VALUES ({});".format(val_str)
print sql_str
```
Database Program/script_005.py

Save the file and run it. Enter the details and then `sql_str` will be printed out. If you used backslashes like me, you may notice that there are long spaces in the SQL command. Don't worry about the spaces; the SQL code will still work correctly.

Note: I have only used backslashes here to make it easier to read in the book, so don't feel you have to!

Double check that the statement looks like this:

```
INSERT INTO SIMPSON_INFO (NAME, GENDER, AGE, OCCUPATION) VALUES ('Bart Simpson', 'Male', 10, 'Student')
```
Reference SQL

If everything worked correctly, we now have an SQL statement that has been created from user inputs. Cool, huh?

Finally, we need execute the SQL and save the changes like so:

```
conn.execute(sql_str)
conn.commit()
print "Number of changes:", conn.total_changes
```

Save the file and run it. Add Bart Simpson to the database with the following details:

Name: Bart Simpson
Gender: Male
Age: 10
Occupation: Student

If everything has been written correctly, then the SQL will run without error and one change will be made to the database. If you get an error, it is likely to be a typo. The SQL string has to be written perfectly to work, so check the commas, quotes, formats etc. I also recommend trying to read the error to see what is going wrong.

Step Three: Viewing All Characters

Before continuing, comment out the line that calls the `newCharacter()` function. We don't want to add a new character in this section.

Let's make a function that collects the data from the table and prints it out. The function will be called `viewAll()` and look like the following:

```
def viewAll():
    # Create sql string
    sql_str = "SELECT * from SIMPSON_INFO"
    cursor = conn.execute(sql_str)
```

Then call the function:

```
viewAll()
```
Database Program/script_007.py

Save the file, run it and check for errors.

We can display the data by using `.fetchall()` and then printing the result.

```
# Get data from cursor in array
rows = cursor.fetchall()
print rows
```
Database Program/script_008.py

Save the file and run it. All the data should be printed out. Good work – that's the `viewAll()` function done.

Step Four: Viewing Specific Characters

We can also make a function that searches for a specific character and then prints out their details. Here is a breakdown of how the function will work:

1. Ask user for the character name
2. Run SQL statement using this name
3. Output results of statement

Asking User for the Character Name

Let's create a new function named `viewDetails()` and then ask the user to input the character's name.

```
def viewDetails():
    print "\nViewing character details"

    # Take name input
    name = raw_input("Enter the character's name: ")
```

```
    print name
```
Database Program/script_009.py

Call the `viewDetails()` function near the bottom of the script, then save the file and run it. Check that the script runs without error.

The SQL Statement
The next step is to make an SQL statement that gets the character's details from the database. The SQL will look something like:

```
SELECT * from SIMPSON_INFO where NAME='Bart Simpson'
```
Reference SQL Code

To make this SQL statement, we can use the `.format()` function to insert the name.

```
sql_str = "SELECT * from SIMPSON_INFO where \
    NAME='{}'".format(name)
print sql_str
```
Database Program/script_010.py

Save the file and run the script. Enter a name and make sure that the outputted SQL statement looks correct. When you are confident that the SQL statement is correct, execute it and print out the results like so:

```
cursor = conn.execute(sql_str)
# Get data in array form
rows = cursor.fetchall()
print rows
```
Database Program/script_011.py

Save the file and run the script. When asked for the name,

enter "Bart Simpson" and hopefully the details will be printed out. If not, double check that "Bart Simpson" is spelled exactly as it appears in the database. Also, the database entries are case sensitive. For example, searching for 'BART SIMPSON' would not find 'Bart Simpson'.

When it works, the details will be printed out like so:

[(1, u'Bart Simpson', u'Male', 11, u'Student')]

Outputting the Data

Printing out the array is a bit messy and not very user friendly. So, let's make a function that takes the data and prints it out in the following way:

Id: 1
Name: Bart Simpson
Gender: Male
Age: 20
Occupation: Student

So, the function needs to take in an array as the parameter and then loop through each row to print out the data. We will call the function `printData()`. Here's the code:

```
def printData(data):
    for row in data:
        print "Id:", row[0]
        print "Name:", row[1]
        print "Gender:", row[2]
        print "Age:", row[3]
        print "Occupation:", row[4], "\n"
```

Database Program/script_012.py

Note: Make sure this function is placed near the top of the script so that the function appears before it is called.

To call the function, change the following in the `viewDetails()` function:

```
print rows
```
Database Program/script_011.py

To:

```
printData(rows)
```
Database Program/script_012.py

Save and run the script. Enter a character name and hopefully the data should be printed out in a nice, organised way. In my opinion, it looks much better!

One More Enhancement

Run the script again and enter a name that is not in the database. The script ends and does not tell the user what happened.

We can fix this by setting up an `if` statement to check if the `rows` array is empty. Add the following to the `viewDetails()` function:

```
if len(rows) == 0:
    # There is no data in array
    print 'No records found'
else:
    # Print the data
    printData(rows)
```
Database Program/script_013.py

Save the file and run it. Now we can enter a name that does not exist in the database and the output will tell us that no records were found. Check that the function still works for characters that exist in the database. Good stuff.

Step Five: Delete a Character

In this part, we are going to make a function that deletes a character. Here is how it will work:

1. Ask user for the character name
2. Run SQL statement using this name
3. Output results of statement
4. Confirm the delete
5. Run delete SQL

Reusing Code

It looks like we need similar functionality to the `viewDetails()` function. So, copy and paste the `viewDetails()` function. Now change the function name and the first line from 'viewing' to 'delete' as shown:

```
def deleteCharacter():
    print "\nDeleting a Character"

    # Take name input
    name = raw_input("Enter the character's name: ")
    sql_str = "SELECT * from SIMPSON_INFO where NAME='{}'"\
        .format(name)

    cursor = conn.execute(sql_str)

    # Get data in array form
```

```
    rows = cursor.fetchall()
    if len(rows) == 0:
        # There is no data in array
        print 'No records found'
    else:
        # Print the data
        printData(rows)
```

Database Program/script_014.py

Comment out any functions that are being called and add the following:

```
deleteCharacter()
```

Database Program/script_014.py

Save the file, run it and check for any errors. If there is a match, we can delete the character.

Problems With Duplicate Character Names

Now, we are going to hit a problem if there are two or more database entries with the same name. To fix this, we can print out the results and then get the user to choose which character they want to delete. So, when duplicate character names exist, we can get the user to input the ID of the character they want to change.

Note: Remember - the ID is unique for every character.

Here is a quick breakdown of what can happen:

1. No results - end the function
2. One result - perfect!
3. More than one result - user enters the character's ID

So, we can get the ID of the character by changing the if

statement in the `deleteCharacter()` function from:

```python
if len(rows) == 0:
    # There is no data in array
    print 'No records found'
else:
    # Print the data
    printData(rows)
```
Database Program/script_014.py

To:

```python
# ID to change
change_id = 0

if len(rows) == 0:
    print 'No records found'
    # End the function
    return
elif len(rows) == 1:
    print 'One record found'
    # Select row
    row = rows[0]
    # Select Id
    change_id = row[0]
    printData(rows)
else:
    print 'More than one record found...'
    printData(rows)
    change_id = raw_input(\
    'Type the ID of the character to update: ')

print "Change ID:", change_id
```
Database Program/script_015.py

Save the file and run the script. Enter a character name that is in the table and check that the `change_id` matches.

Note: If you don't currently have a duplicate character, run the newCharacter() *function and create a character with the same name.*

Time to see what happens when we hit duplicate character names. Try running the script again and enter the character's name that exists twice in the database. Both sets of details should be printed out and the program should ask you to input the character ID. Enter an ID and voila, we have a row ID to edit.

Deleting the Character
Before deleting the character, we should confirm that the user wants to delete the character.

```
delete=raw_input("Confirm character delete (y/n): ")
```
Database Program/script_016.py

To check whether the user inputted "y", we need to create another if statement.

```
if delete == "y":
    sql_str = "DELETE from SIMPSON_INFO where ID={}"\
        .format(change_id)
    conn.execute(sql_str)
    conn.commit()
    print "Number of changes: ", conn.total_changes
```
Database Program/script_017.py

Save the file and run it. Enter a characters name, type "y", and the character should be deleted. Run the script again and enter the same character's name. Only one character with that name should be shown. Great work!

Putting it all Together

Let's create a user interface that makes it easy for the user to add, view and delete a character. It will print out some options and ask the user what they want to do, like so:

```
def options():
    # Print out the options
    print '\nWhat would you like to do?'
    print '1. Add a new character'
    print '2. View all characters'
    print '3. Search for a character'
    print '4. Delete a character'
    print '5. Exit'

    # Ask user what they want to do
    response = raw_input('Enter number: ')
```
Database Program/script_018.py

Make sure to call the `options()` function at the bottom of the script:

```
options()
```
Database Program/script_018.py

Save the file, run it and check for errors.

To make the correct function run for the value the user has inputted, we can use an `if` statement like so:

```
if response == '1':
    newCharacter()
elif response == '2':
    viewAll()
elif response == '3':
    viewDetails()
elif response == '4':
    deleteCharacter()
else:
    print 'Exiting the program'
    return
```
Database Program/script_019.py

Save the file and run it. Go through each response and check all the options are working correctly.

There is one final enhancement we can make for the user. At the moment, they have to keep running the script again every time they want to do something. To fix this, we can create a loop that asks the user if they want to do something else after the `options()` function has finished. A `while` loop is perfect for this:

```
def mainLoop():
    in_loop = True
    while in_loop == True:
        # Run options function
        options()
        # Ask user if they want to continue
        again = raw_input(\
        'Would you like to do something else? (y/n)\
')
        # if answer does not equal 'y', exit loop
        if again != 'y':
            in_loop = False
```

Before running the script, change the call for `options()` to `mainLoop()` at the bottom of the script. Also make sure that the `mainLoop()` function is below the `options()` function.

Save the file and run it. Enter option number "2" or "5" to avoid entering any details. A prompt will be shown asking if you want to continue. If you enter "y", the loop should continue. If you enter anything else, it should exit. Did it work? If so, nice one!

Wrapping Up

We have created a pretty cool program here that can modify information in a database through a user interface. We have created functions to create a new table, add characters, view specific characters and even delete them. We then created a main user interface so that the user can easily chose what they want to do. And all of this through the Python shell and user inputs!

BONUS! I have created a chapter extra to show you how to update a character using user inputs.

Sounds good? You can sign up and download it from here:

http://www.inadaybooks.com/scripts/

Python GUI's: Installation

"An interface is humane if it is responsive to human needs and considerate of human frailties"
- Jef Raskin, Human-Computer Interface Expert

What is a GUI?

GUI stands for Graphical User Interface. The programs you commonly use on your computer have a GUI with some code behind them that makes everything work. To make a GUI using Python, we are going to use a toolkit called wxPython.

Installation

Fortunately, wxPython is super easy to install. Go to the following webpage:

> http://inadaybooks.com/wxpython

For Windows

Look for the 'Windows Binaries' header and then you should see some download links. Find the file that looks like this:

wxPython3.0-win32-py27

If you don't know what version of Python you have, try downloading the 32-bit version of wxPython first. If it does not work after installation, try downloading the 64-bit version.

When the file has downloaded, double click it and go through the installation.

To check that it worked, open up IDLE or a Python shell and run the following command:

```
import wx
```

If wxPython installed correctly, then no errors will appear.

For Mac
Look for 'Mac OSX Binaries' and then download the cocoa file. It should look something like this:

wxPython3.0-osx-cocoa-py2.7

When it has finished downloading, open the file and then go through the installation process. When you complete the installation, open up IDLE or a Python shell and run the following command:

```
import wx
```

If wxPython has installed correctly, then no errors will appear.

For Linux

Open up the terminal and then enter the following commands (You can copy and paste these commands from the In A Day Books website):

```
$ wget http://inadaybooks.com/wxPython-3.0.tar.bz2
$ tar xvjf wxPython-3.0.tar.bz2
$ cd wxPython-3.0/
$ mkdir bld
$ cd wxPython/
$ sudo checkinstall -y --pkgname=wxpython --pkgversion=3.0.0 --pkgrelease=1 --pkglicense=wxWidgets --pkgsource=http://www.wxpython.org/ --maintainer=reingart@gmail.com --requires=python-wxversion,python2.7,python -D python build-wxpython.py --build_dir=../bld --install
```

When wxPython has finished installing, we can check the installation by entering the following commands:

```
$ python
>>> import wx
```

If no errors appear, then wxPython has successfully installed.

GUI's: Creating Your First GUI With wxPython

"The rise of Google, the rise of Facebook, the rise of Apple, I think are proof that there is a place for computer science as something that solves problems that people face every day."
- Eric Schmidt, CEO of Google

Introduction to wxPython

Learning the Basics

Create a new Python file and then import the wxPython module.

```
import wx
```

gui/script_001.py

Now add the following:

```
app = wx.App()
frame = wx.Frame(None, title="Python GUI", \
   size=(300,200))
frame.Show()
app.MainLoop()
```

gui/script_002.py

Every wxPython application needs that code. Allow me to take you through it:

Line 1

- `wx.App()` creates the application object.
- This is required for every program you make using wxPython.

Line 2

- `wx.Frame()` creates a window.
- This is like every other window you use on a computer.

Line 3

- `.Show()` makes the frame appear on the screen.

Line 4

- `.MainLoop` handles all the events such as clicking or scrolling.

Save the file and run it. A window should appear on the screen. It has the title and the close, minimise and maximise buttons. Just like any other window! Cool huh?

To change the title of the window, you can change the `title` parameter in the `wx.Frame()` function. You can also change the size of the window using the `size` parameter.

The Class System

We will use the class system to add content to the frame. Stay with me, this is easier than it sounds! To create exactly the same window using the class system, we need to change the script to the following:

```
import wx

class Frame(wx.Frame):
    def __init__(self):
        wx.Frame.__init__(self, None,\
        title="Python GUI", size=(300,200))

app = wx.App()
frame = Frame()
frame.Show()
app.MainLoop()
```

gui/script_003.py

Note: Don't miss the `frame = Frame()` *change near the bottom of the script.*

This looks like a complete mess with all the `__init__`'s and `self`'s. Try not to worry about them too much; you will get the hang of it as the chapter goes on.

Save the file and run it. The window should look exactly the same as before.

So that you can see out how this is working, we will pass some text into the `Frame` class and make it the title of the window. So, modify the `__init__` function and add title as the second parameter and then make the title equal to that variable. Here is the code:

```
import wx

class Frame(wx.Frame):
    # Added title parameter
    def __init__(self, title):
        # title = title variable
        wx.Frame.__init__(self, None,\
            title=title, size=(300,200))

app = wx.App()
# Pass in the frame title
frame = Frame("Python GUI")
frame.Show()
app.MainLoop()
```

gui/script_004.py

Save the file and run it. If all went well, then perfect!

Cool Stuff: Aligning the Window

To align the window in the center of the screen, add `self.Center()` to the __init__ function.

To make the window appear in a certain point on the screen, we can use `self.Move((600,400))`. In this example, the 'x' coordinate is 600 and the 'y' coordinate is 400.

Adding a Button

Before adding a button, we need to add a panel. This is basically a container that groups things such as buttons and text.

```
panel = wx.Panel(self)
```

gui/script_005.py

Then we can add a button to the `panel` using the `wx.Button()` function like so:

```
button = wx.Button(panel,label="Exit", \
   size=(100,40),pos=(100,30))
```

gui/script_006.py

So, here is what's happening:

- The button is being placed in the `panel`.
- The `label` is the text that appears on the button.
- The `size` is the size of the button.
- The `pos` is the position of the button in the panel.

Save the file and run it. You should see a button that you can click. The button doesn't do anything at the moment, but it still works like a button!

Let's make the button shut down the GUI. To do this, we need to tell wxPython to run a function when the button is clicked. We do this by using the `.Bind` function like so:

```
# Bind button event to the function self.exit
button.Bind(wx.EVT_BUTTON, self.exit)
```

gui/script_007.py

So, when the button is clicked (the event), the function `self.exit` is run.

Save the file and run it. Gah! You should get an error like so:

```
'Frame' object has no attribute 'exit'
```

To fix this, we need to create a function named `exit()` in the `Frame()` class. The function needs to take the parameters `self` and `event`. The `event` parameter will contain details of the event that we can access in the function. Add the following just below the __init__ function:

```
def exit(self, event):
    self.Destroy()
```

gui/script_008.py

Note: Make sure that you don't put this inside the __init__ function.

If you are stuck or unsure how the code supposed to look, take a look at the scripts that can be found online at:

http://www.InADayBooks.com

Save the file and run it. Now click the button. If the program closed, give yourself a hearty pat on the back! You now know how to make buttons do stuff!

Menus

Creating a Menu Bar

If you look at the top left hand side of a window, you will see some menu items such as File, Edit and Help. If you are using Mac, they are located in the top left of the screen. Anyway, we are going to make our very own one of those. Pretty awesome, right? Add the following to the __init__ function:

```
# Create menu bar
menuBar = wx.MenuBar()
# Create the menus
fileMenu = wx.Menu()
editMenu = wx.Menu()
```

gui/script_009.py

Save the file and run it. Can you see the menu bar? I can't. Well, we can fix this by setting the menu bar as the `menuBar` object like so:

```
self.SetMenuBar(menuBar)
```

gui/script_010.py

Save the file and run it. Well, that's annoying. There is still no menu bar. This is where we scratch our heads and wonder what's happening. And then we realise that we never linked `fileMenu` and `editMenu` with the menu bar! We can add menus to `menuBar` using the `.Append()` function like so:

```
# Add fileMenu and editMenu to menuBar
menuBar.Append(fileMenu, "File")
menuBar.Append(editMenu, "Edit")
```

gui/script_011.py

Save the file and run it. Woah! Our menu items finally appear!

Try clicking on the menu items. They don't contain anything. Let's add "New File", "Open" and "Exit" to the `file` menu, and just like the menu bar, we use `.Append()` to do this:

```
# Add items to fileMenu
fileMenu.Append(wx.NewId(), "New File")
fileMenu.Append(wx.NewId(), "Open")
fileMenu.Append(wx.NewId(), "Exit")
```

gui/script_012.py

Save the file and run it. Click on the file menu and you should see the items. Nifty, huh? Go ahead and add your own items to the Edit menu.

The Status Bar

We can add functionality so that when the user hovers over a menu item, a short description is shown. To do this, add a status bar to the __init__ function like so:

```
self.CreateStatusBar()
```
gui/script_013.py

Save the file and run the script. Take a look at the bottom of the window and there should be a small bar. This is the status bar.

To add a description to one of the menu items, we need to change the following:

```
fileMenu.Append(wx.NewId(), "New File")
```
gui/script_013.py

To:

```
fileMenu.Append(wx.NewId(), "New File", \
  "Create a new file")
```
gui/script_014.py

Save the file and run it. Now go to File and then hover over the New File item. You should see that "Create a new file" appears in the status bar at the bottom of the window. Good stuff.

Adding Events To Menu Items

Try clicking 'File – New File'. Nothing happens, right? To fix this, we have to bind the menu item to an event and function just like we did with the button.

Let's make the Exit menu item actually exit the program.

First, we need to create a reference to the Exit menu item by changing:

```
fileMenu.Append(wx.NewId(), "Exit")
```
gui/script_014.py

To:

```
exitItem = fileMenu.Append(wx.NewId(), "Exit")
```
gui/script_015.py

We can bind the exit item to the `exit` function we created earlier. The event for clicking on an item in the menu is `wx.EVT_MENU`. The following code is a little different to binding a button, but it works in the same way.

```
# Bind exit menu item to exit function
self.Bind(wx.EVT_MENU, self.exit, exitItem)
```
gui/script_016.py

Save the file and run it. Go to 'File – Quit' and the program will exit. Nice one.

Widgets

wxPython Widgets

This section contains some of the commonly used wxPython widgets. There are more and they can be found on the following page:

http://inadaybooks.com/wxpythonwidgets

wx.StaticText

Figure 8.1 shows the static text widget.

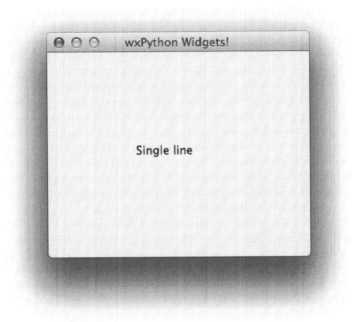

Figure 8.1: Static Text

Static text can be added like so:

```
wx.StaticText(panel, label='Single line', \
    pos=(100,100))
```

gui/widgets_001.py

wx.StaticBox

Figure 8.2 shows the static box widget.

Figure 8.2: Static Box

A static box can be used to group different widgets on the screen. Here's the code:

```
wx.StaticBox(panel, label='Static Box Title', \
  pos=(10,10), size=(280,200))
wx.StaticText(panel, label='Single line', \
  pos=(100,100))
```

gui/widgets_002.py

wx.ComboBox

Figure 8.3 shows the combo box widget.

Figure 8.3: Combo Box

As shown above, a combo box shows a list of items. Here is how you can create your own:

```
simpsons =['Bart', 'Lisa', 'Maggie', 'Marge', 'Homer']
cb = wx.ComboBox(panel, pos=(100, 50), \
    choices=simpsons)
```

gui/widgets_003.py

Save the file and run it. Click on the down arrow and the characters from the array will appear. If you click on the character's name, you will notice that it can be edited. To change this, add `style=wx.CB_READONLY` like so:

```
cb = wx.ComboBox(panel, pos=(100, 50), \
    choices=simpsons, style=wx.CB_READONLY)
```
gui/widgets_003.py

Save the file and run it. You won't be able to enter any text now.

wx.CheckBox

Figure 8.4 shows the checkbox widget.

Figure 8.4: Checkbox

Checkboxes are pretty simple to add:

```
wx.CheckBox(panel, label='Male', pos=(100, 50))
wx.CheckBox(panel, label='Female', pos=(100, 80))
```
gui/widgets_004.py

wx.RadioButton

Figure 8.5 shows the radio button widget.

Figure 8.5: Radio Button

Radio buttons are created like so:

```
wx.RadioButton(panel, label='Male', pos=(100, 50), \
   style=wx.RB_GROUP)
wx.RadioButton(panel, label='Female', pos=(100, 80))
```
gui/widgets_005.py

wx.TextCtrl

Figure 8.6 shows the text control widget for single and multiple lines.

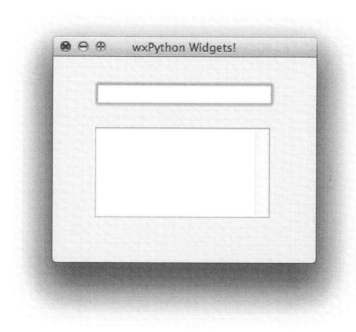

Figure 8.6: Text Control

So this widget allows the user to input some text.

`wx.TextCtrl(panel, size=(300, -1), pos=(100,270))`

gui/widgets_006.py

Note: The value "-1" has been used as the height to set the text control at the default height. This allows you to change the width and keep the default height.

We can get multiple lines of text by using `style=wx.TE_MULTILINE` like so:

```
wx.TextCtrl(panel, style=wx.TE_MULTILINE, \
    size=(300, 200), pos=(100,50))
```

gui/widgets_006.py

wx.SpinCtrl

Figure 8.7 shows the spin control widget.

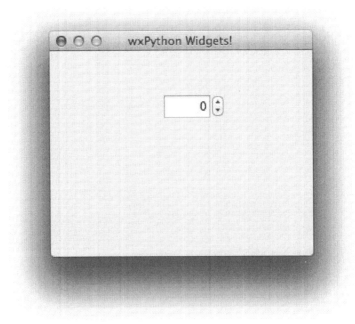

Figure 8.7: Spin Control

Spin Control allows you to increment and decrement numbers. Here's how you can add them:

```
wx.SpinCtrl(panel, value='0', pos=(130, 50), \
    size=(70, 25))
```

gui/widgets_007.py

Events for the Widgets

Widget	Event	Description
wx.Button	EVT_BUTTON	When a button is clicked
wx.ComboBox	EVT_COMBOBOX	When an item in the list is selected
wx.CheckBox	EVT_CHECKBOX	When a checkbox is clicked
wx.RadioButton	EVT_RADIOBUTTON	When a radio button is clicked

The widgets wx.StaticText, wx.StaticBox and wx.TextCtrl do not have any events.

Note: You can search Google to find the events for other widgets. Type "wxpython" with the widget name and then "event".

An Awesome Spin Control Example

In this example, we are going to use a spin control to change the label of some static text.

Firstly, we need to create the spin control and static text. I have used `self.valueText` to make the static text a global variable. This means we can access the static text in other functions. Don't worry, this will all become clear soon. Promise! Add the following to the __init__ function:

```
sc = wx.SpinCtrl(panel, value='0', pos=(130, 50), \
    size=(70, 25))
self.valueText = wx.StaticText(panel, label='', \
    pos=(130,80))
```

gui/widgets_008.py

Note: You can get the file from the website if you are not sure how the script is supposed to look.

Save the file and run it. The spin control should appear in the window.

Next, we need to bind the spin control to run a function when its value has changed. The function will be called `self.spinControl`, so we can bind the spin control event like so:

```
sc.Bind(wx.EVT_SPINCTRL, self.spinControl)
```

gui/widgets_009.py

And here is the `spinControl()` function (make sure you put this outside of the __init__ function:

```
def spinControl(self, event):
    # Get spin control value
    value = event.GetPosition()
    # Update static text
    self.valueText.SetLabel(str(value))
```

gui/widgets_009.py

The `event.GetPosition()` looks up the current value in the spin control. The label of `self.valueText` was then set to this value. Because we made the static text a global object, we were able to update it easily in this function.

Note: If you want to find what is passed into the function for different types of events, Google it!

Save the file and run it. Play with the spin control and you should see the value change in the static text. Now that is cool!

A Quick Summary of Objects, Binds and Events

The event is what the user does to a widget, e.g. a click.

To link an event and a widget together, we use the `Bind` function.

When an event happens, `Bind` calls the function we specified.

Wrapping Up

In this chapter we have gone through some of the basics of wxPython. It's pretty cool that we can create programs that look and behave exactly like the ones we use every day. We have made buttons do stuff, added a menu bar and changed static text depending on the value of a spin control. We have also been introduced to some of the most common wxPython widgets.

GUI Program: An Epic Program that Connect GUI's and Databases

"All of my friends who have younger siblings who are going to college or high school - my number one piece of advice is: You should learn how to program."
- Mark Zuckerberg, Co-Founder of Facebook

The Objective

We are about to make a super awesome GUI for the database program we created previously. Don't worry if you did not complete the chapter - the script is available from the In A Day Books website.

Also note that this program requires SQLite to be installed. So if you haven't installed it, go to the installation chapter for Databases and do it now.

The GUI will need to do the following:

1. Let the user add a new character
2. Show all the characters in the table on the right hand side
3. Make it easy to delete characters

This means that we need the following functions from the database program:

- newCharacter()
- viewAll()
- deleteCharacter()

Using these requirements, I have drawn up a wireframe of the GUI:

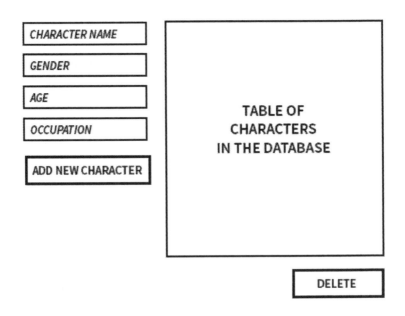

Modifying the Database Program

There are a few changes that we need to make to the database program before using it for the GUI. All of the inputs will be entered through the GUI instead of the Python shell, so we need to remove the `raw_input`'s and change them to parameters in the function. For example, the beginning of the `newCharacter()` function needs to be changed from:

```
def newCharacter():
    print '\nAdding a new character...'

    # Take inputs
    name = raw_input('Name: ')
    gender = raw_input('Gender: ')
    age = raw_input('Age: ')
    occupation = raw_input('Occupation: ')
```

Database code from earlier

To:

```
def newCharacter(name, gender, age, occupation):
    # Changes: takes details as inputs.
    print '\nAdding a new character...'
```

gui-simpson/db_program.py

The functions also need to return certain values. I recommend grabbing the file that I have converted from the website. It will save you a few headaches! It is called `db_program.py` and can be found in the scripts for this chapter. I have made a detailed change log that you can view on the website if you want to know what has changed.

http://www.InADayBooks.com/scripts

The First GUI Steps

Starter GUI Code

Let's start with some familiar GUI code. Create a new Python file and then add the following code: (If you don't want to write out all this code, you can get it from the In A Day Books website.)

```python
import wx

class Frame(wx.Frame):
    def __init__(self, title):
        wx.Frame.__init__(self, None,\
            title=title, size=(800,600))
        panel = wx.Panel(self)

        # Creating the menu bar
        menuBar = wx.MenuBar()
        fileMenu = wx.Menu()
        exitItem = fileMenu.Append(wx.NewId(), "Exit")
        menuBar.Append(fileMenu, "File")

        self.SetMenuBar(menuBar)
        self.Bind(wx.EVT_MENU,         self.exitProgram, exitItem)

        self.CreateStatusBar()

    def exitProgram(self, event):
        self.Destroy()

app = wx.App()
frame = Frame("Python GUI")
frame.Show()
app.MainLoop()
```

gui-simpson/script_001.py

Note: If you are using previous code, make sure to change the window size to 800x600.

Save the file and run it. Check that no errors appear and that you can exit the program from the file menu. Good.

Importing db_program.py

The program that has been slightly modified from the database program is called `db_program.py`. To use the functions from `db_program.py`, we need to import it as a module. Make sure that `db_program.py` is in the same folder as the GUI script that you are working on and then modify:

```
import wx
```
gui-simpson/script_001.py

To:

```
import wx, db_program
```
gui-simpson/script_002.py

Save the file and run it. If an error is returned, check the spelling of the module name and that db_program.py is in the same folder as the script you are running.

Adding a Character

The Interface

The 'Add New Character' section of the user interface should look something like the following:

Add a New Character

Character Name:

Gender:

Age:

Occupation:

Add Character

Let's make the basic outline first by adding the text and buttons to the __init__ function like so:

```
# Setup Add New Character UI
# Text at the top
wx.StaticText(panel, label='Add a new character',
pos=(30,40))

# Text for name, gender etc
wx.StaticText(panel, label='Name:', pos=(30,70))
wx.StaticText(panel, label='Gender:', pos=(30,110))
wx.StaticText(panel, label='Age:', pos=(30,150))
wx.StaticText(panel, label='Occupation:', \
   pos=(30,190))

# Single line text boxes
wx.TextCtrl(panel, size=(150, -1), pos=(130,70))
wx.TextCtrl(panel, size=(150, -1), pos=(130,110))
wx.TextCtrl(panel, size=(150, -1), pos=(130,150))
wx.TextCtrl(panel, size=(150, -1), pos=(130,190))
```

gui-simpson/script_003.py

Note: It looks like a lot to write but it is mainly copying, pasting and editing a few values.

Save the file and run it. Check it looks like the wireframe.

We can make this section a bit neater by adding a static box to group the widgets. Change:

```
# Text at the top
wx.StaticText(panel, label='Add a new character', \
    pos=(30,40))
```
gui-simpson/script_003.py

To:

```
# Create static box
wx.StaticBox(panel, label='Add a new character', \
  pos=(20,40), size=(280,190))
```
gui-simpson/script_004.py

Save the file and run it. Feel free to change the positions, text and sizing until you are happy. The GUI should look something like this:

Adding The Button

The next thing is to create a button that adds the character to the database. We will bind the button to a function called addCharacter() like so:

```
# Save button
save = wx.Button(panel, label="Add Character", \
    pos=(100, 230))
save.Bind(wx.EVT_BUTTON, self.addCharacter)
```
gui-simpson/script_005.py

Before running the script, we need to create the addCharacter() function. Place the following outside of the __init__ function:

```
def addCharacter(self, event):
    pass
```
gui-simpson/script_005.py

Save the file and run it. The button should appear.

To add the character to the database, we need the inputs from the text boxes. We can access these inputs in the addCharacter() function by changing the following text controls to global variables:

```
wx.TextCtrl(panel, size=(150, -1), pos=(130,70))
wx.TextCtrl(panel, size=(150, -1), pos=(130,110))
wx.TextCtrl(panel, size=(150, -1), pos=(130,150))
wx.TextCtrl(panel, size=(150, -1), pos=(130,190))
```
gui-simpson/script_005.py

Change to:

```
self.sName = wx.TextCtrl(panel, size=(150, -1), \
    pos=(130,70))
self.sGen = wx.TextCtrl(panel, size=(150, -1), \
    pos=(130,110))
self.sAge = wx.TextCtrl(panel, size=(150, -1), \
    pos=(130,150))
self.sOcc = wx.TextCtrl(panel, size=(150, -1), \
    pos=(130,190))
```

gui-simpson/script_006.py

Note: The 's' is short for Simpson!

To get the text out of the text controls, we can use the `.GetValue()` function. Delete "pass" from the `addCharacter()` function and add the following:

```
name = self.sName.GetValue()
gen = self.sGen.GetValue()
age = self.sAge.GetValue()
occ = self.sOcc.GetValue()

print name
print gen
print age
print occ
```

gui-simpson/script_006.py

Save the file and run it. Enter some data in the text boxes and click 'Add Character'. The data should get outputted in the shell. Pretty cool, huh?

Adding the Character
To add a character to the database, we can use the `newCharacter()` function from the `db_program` module.

The `newCharacter()` function takes the name, gender, age and occupation as parameters. So, to add a new character to the database, we need to pass the user's inputted values into the `newCharacter()` function. To check that the character was added successfully, we will use the `viewAll()` function. Add the following to the `addCharacter()` function:

```
# Adding character to database
db_program.newCharacter(name, gen, age, occ)
print db_program.viewAll()
```

gui-simpson/script_007.py

Save the file and run it. Add some data to the boxes and click 'Add Character'. If an error was returned, it could be because you entered letters into the 'Age' box. For age, only numbers are allowed.

If the character was added successfully, then perfect!

Bullet Proofing The User Inputs

There are a couple of problems we need to fix:

1. The user can enter letters into the age text box.
2. The program will add a character if one or more of the text controls are left blank.

Problem 1: The Age Input Allows Non-Integer Values

If you have not entered a letter in the Age text box, try it now and click the 'Add Character' button. An SQL error will be returned.

To fix this, we could use a spin control widget as it only allows integers. So, change the following:

```
self.sAge = wx.TextCtrl(panel, size=(150, -1), \
  pos=(130,150))
```

gui-simpson/script_007.py

To:

```
self.sAge = wx.SpinCtrl(panel, value='0', \
  pos=(130, 150), size=(70, 25))
```

gui-simpson/script_008.py

Save the file and run it. You should see that a spin control has replaced the text box. Try entering some text and check that it is not allowed. Problem solved.

Problem 2: Empty Text Inputs

All of the inputs should be checked that they contain a value before adding the character to the database. To do this, we can use an `if` statement that looks at each variable for blank values. So, add the following to the `addCharacter()` function just after the `self.sOcc.GetValue()` line:

```
# Checking if variables have a value
if (name == '') or (gen == '') \
  or (age == '') or (occ == ''):
    print 'At least one variable is empty'
    return False
```

gui-simpson/script_009.py

Save the file and run it. Leave some of the text boxes blank and then click 'Add Character'. Check the output and you should see the message that at least one variable is empty. Just what we wanted! It can catch empty user inputs. Problem 2 ticked off!

Note: `return False` *ends the function.*

Improving the User Experience

Message Dialogs

Imagine that you are the user and you click 'Add Character'. Nothing happens. Not one single thing. How do you know that you are doing something wrong?

Instead of printing some text to the Python shell, we can alert the user in the GUI using dialogs. They are basically popups for the program and look something like this:

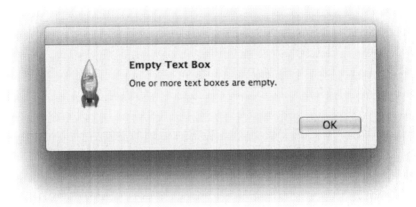

The code to make it appear looks like this:

```
dlg = wx.MessageDialog(None, 'Some Help Text',\
    'Title', wx.OK)
dlg.ShowModal()
dlg.Destroy()
```

Example Code

Here's how the code is working:

1. The `wx.MessageDialog()` is used to create a message dialog object. It takes parameters such as the title and

some message text.

2. The `wx.OK` is the dialog style that displays the 'OK' button. To add a 'Cancel' button, you can write `wx.OK|wx.CANCEL` as the style.

You can see what other styles there are at the following link:

<u>http://inadaybooks.com/msgdialog</u>

Let's add a dialog message that tells the user that they need to input data into each text box. Change:

```
print 'At least one variable is empty'
```
gui-simpson/script_009.py

To:

```
# Alert user that a variable is empty
dlg = wx.MessageDialog(None, \
    'Some character details are missing.\
    Enter values in each text box.',\
    'Missing Details', wx.OK)
dlg.ShowModal()
dlg.Destroy()
```
gui-simpson/script_010.py

Note: I recommend putting the Message Dialog code all on one line. Unfortunately, there is not really enough space in the book to do this!

Save the file and run it. Leave a text box empty and click 'Add Character'. A message dialog should appear to stop you entering a character.

Resetting The Inputs

When a new character has been added, it would be helpful if the text controls were cleared and the age reset to zero. This the process of adding multiple characters quicker because the user does not have to keep deleting the previous character's details. Add the following to the end of the `addCharacter` function:

```
# Empty text boxes when finished.
self.sName.Clear()
self.sGen.Clear()
self.sOcc.Clear()
```

gui-simpson/script_011.py

Save the file and run it. Enter some details and click 'Add Character'. The text controls should get emptied after the character has been added. Result!

To set the age back to zero, add the following:

```
self.sAge.SetValue(0)
```

gui-simpson/script_011.py

Save the file and run it. Change the age value and enter some details. Click 'Add Character' and the age value should be reset to zero.

Table Time

Table Setup

We are going to show all of the characters from the database in a table. To do this, we will use the list control widget. In the `__init__` function, add the following:

```
# Setup the Table UI
# Setup table as listCtrl
listCtrl = wx.ListCtrl(panel, size=(400,400),\
  pos=(350,40), style=wx.LC_REPORT |wx.BORDER_SUNKEN)
```
gui-simpson/script_012.py

The `wx.ListCtrl` widget takes the size and position parameters. The style parameter looks strange, but it is required to show the list control. Don't worry about the style too much; just make sure you use it.

Save the file and run it. There should be a big blank square on the right hand side of the window.

Let's add columns to the list control for each detail about the characters. To add a column to the table, the `.InsertColumn()` function is used. It takes two parameters - the first is the column number and the second is the column title. Add the following code just below the `listCtrl` object:

```
# Add columns to listCtrl
listCtrl.InsertColumn(0, "ID")
listCtrl.InsertColumn(1, "Name")
listCtrl.InsertColumn(2, "Gender")
listCtrl.InsertColumn(3, "Age")
listCtrl.InsertColumn(4, "Occupation")
```
gui-simpson/script_013.py

Save the file and run it again. Wooo! You should see the five columns in the table!

Inserting Data Into The Table

Here's what we have to do to insert data:

1. Get the data from the database
2. Add it to the list control

Hmm, that doesn't sound so difficult! Let's make a function that fills the list control. The function starts like so:

```
# Get data from the database
def fillListCtrl(self):
    allData = db_program.viewAll()
```
gui-simpson/script_014.py

Note: Make sure this new function is outside of the __init__ function.

To add a row of data to the list control, the .Append() function is used. We can loop through our data and append each row like so:

```
for row in allData:
    # Loop though and append data
    listCtrl.Append(row)
```
gui-simpson/script_015.py

Before running the script, call `fillListCtrl()` in the __init__ function.

```
# Add data to the list control
self.fillListCtrl()
```
gui-simpson/script_015.py

Save the file and run the script. Okay, I get an error saying the 'listCtrl' is not defined.

To fix this, we need to make the `listCtrl` object global so that we can access it in other functions. So, change every variable in the script that is:

`listCtrl`

gui-simpson/script_015.py

To:

`self.listCtrl`

gui-simpson/script_016.py

This includes changing the `listCtrl` object and where the columns are created. The other place is in the `fillListCtrl()` function where the rows are being appended. See the files on the website if you are unsure.

http://inadaybooks.com/scripts

Save the file and run it. Boom! Look at that. All of the database information now appears in the list control!

Refreshing The Table When A New Character Is Added

Try adding a new character to the database.

Now take a look at the list control on the right hand side. It doesn't change. We can fix this by calling `fillListCtrl()` at the end of the `addCharacter()` function:

```
# Update list control
self.fillListCtrl()
```

gui-simpson/script_017.py

Save the file and run it. Try adding a new character. Well, it works, sort of. The new character gets added, but all of the other characters get added again to the list control.

To solve this problem, we can delete the current data in the list control and then add the new data. Add the following code to the `fillListCtrl()` function, just before the loop:

```
# Delete old data before adding new data
self.listCtrl.DeleteAllItems()
```

gui-simpson/script_018.py

Save the file and run the script. Add a new character. It works a charm!

Deleting Characters From The Database

Making a Delete Button

It would be great if the user could click on a character in the list control, click a delete button and then the character gets deleted from the database.

Let's do exactly that! The first step is to make a delete button. Add the following to the __init__ function:

```
# Setup a delete button
deleteBtn = wx.Button(panel, label="Delete", \
    pos=(640, 450))
```

gui-simpson/script_019.py

Save the file and run it. Feel free to adjust the position and size of the button.

To delete a character, we need to use the `deleteCharacter()` function from the `db_program` module. This function takes the character ID deletes it from the database. Therefore, our target is to find the ID of the selected row.

Finding the Character ID

To get the character's ID, we will start off by using the `wx.EVT_LIST_ITEM_SELECTED` event. As you may have guessed, this event is triggered when the user clicks on the list control. The event contains details of the selected row, which we can extract.

We need to bind the event to the list control and make it run the function `onSelect`. Add the following to the `__init__` function:

```
# Run onSelect function when item is selected
self.listCtrl.Bind(wx.EVT_LIST_ITEM_SELECTED, \
    self.onSelect)
```

gui-simpson/script_020.py

Now create the function `onSelect` outside of the `__init__` function:

```
def onSelect(self, event):
    pass
```

gui-simpson/script_020.py

Save the file and run it. Click on a row and check that Python does not return any errors.

To get the text in the first column of the row from the event, we can change:

```
pass
```

gui-simpson/script_020.py

To:

```
print event.GetText()
```
gui-simpson/script_021.py

Save the file and run it. Try clicking on the rows in the list control. The ID of the selected row should be printed out for you. We did it!

Now, we can make the ID of the selected row a global variable so that we can easily access it in the delete function. Change the following:

```
print event.GetText()
```
gui-simpson/script_021.py

To:

```
# Get the id of the selected row
self.selectedId = event.GetText()
```
gui-simpson/script_022.py

Save the file and run it. Check there are no errors.

Deleting the Character
Final step! Let's make the button actually delete the selected character. We need to bind the delete button so that when it's clicked, the `onDelete()` function is called. Write the following in the `__init__` function, just after the delete button has been created:

```
# Bind delete button to onDelete function
deleteBtn.Bind(wx.EVT_BUTTON, self.onDelete)
```
gui-simpson/script_023.py

The next step is to create the `onDelete()` function. It will use the `deleteCharacter()` function from the `db_program` module and look like so:

```
def onDelete(self, event):
    # Delete the character
    db_program.deleteCharacter(self.selectedId)
```
gui-simpson/script_023.py

Save the file and run it. Try deleting a character. Hmm, nothing seems to happen. Let's try refreshing the table by calling `self.fillListCtrl()` after deleting a character.

```
# Refresh the table
self.fillListCtrl()
```
gui-simpson/script_024.py

Save the file and run it. Try selecting a row and then clicking delete. YES! It works!

Wrapping Up

Well, that brings this monster chapter to an end. I hope you managed to stick through it and enjoyed it! Really, really good job if you did. We now have a GUI that allows us to add characters, view them and delete them very easily. I would love to keep adding features, but after all, this book is meant to teach you Python In A Day!

Here's a couple of things you could do to make this program even more awesome:

1. Create radio buttons or checkboxes for the gender.
2. Add update character functionality

BONUS! I have created a chapter extra to show you how to easily update a character by adding a couple of new features to the GUI.

Sounds good? You can sign up and download it from here:

http://www.inadaybooks.com/scripts/

Please let me know how far you take this program or if you have any other great ideas or need some help. You can contact me at rich@inadaybooks.com. I will do my best to reply quickly!

Thank You!

I want to say a massive thank you for taking the time to read the book. I hope you got some really useful things out of it, had some fun and can now do some more programming in Python.

So, where do you go from here?

If you haven't already, you could download the chapter extras that add features to each program. Or perhaps you could make your own incredible GUI or scrape a website for some data. When you get stuck, really stuck, I recommend searching on Google or looking in this book for the answer. Creating your own programs is a great way to solidify your knowledge and discover new things about Python.

What to do next?

I have thoroughly enjoyed writing the book, and I hope you enjoyed reading it too. If you feel like the book was worthwhile to you, then please could you help me out and leave a quick review on Amazon? Every review really does help.

If you ever need to reach me to ask any questions, have feedback or suggestions for the book, please get in touch by emailing me at:

rich@inadaybooks.com

Once again, **thank you** for purchasing this book!

Web Scraping Quick Reference

Importing BeautifulSoup
```
from bs4 import BeautifulSoup
```

Opening a webpage
The webpage address is placed where "url" is.
```
webpage = urllib2.urlopen("url")
```

Convert to BeautifulSoup
Converts a "urlopen" object to BeautifulSoup.
```
soup = BeautifulSoup(webpage)
```

BeautifulSoup Cheats
Return the title of the websites:
```
soup.title
```

Return the content inside the body tags:
```
soup.body
```

Return the content inside the head tags:
```
soup.head
```

Prints out the webpage source code with good formatting. It adds indents and line breaks in the correct places:

```
soup.prettify()
```

Searching within the HTML Code
The following finds the first instance of a "div" that has the id "container".

Note: You can swap div for any other tag, such as "a" or

"table". Also, "id" can be swapped for "class", "style" etc.
```
soup.find("div", {"id":"container"})
```

Finds all instances of "div" with the id "container". Same rules apply as the mklbtsoup.find()mkrbt function.
```
soup.findAll("div", {"id":"container"})
```

Extracting Text
Returns the string of text between HTML tags.
```
get_text()
```

Databases Quick Reference

Creating/Connecting to a Database
`conn = sqlite3.connect("database_name")`

Adding a Table
```
CREATE TABLE if not exists table_name
(
Table info goes here
)
```

Here's the example from the book:
```
CREATE TABLE SIMPSON_INFO (
ID INT PRIMARY KEY,
NAME TEXT,
AGE INT
)
```

The five column types are:
INTEGER, NUMERIC, REAL, TEXT and NONE

SQL in Python
Run all SQL statements like so:
`conn.execute("SQL statement here")`

To save any changes you make to the database:
`conn.commit()`

Adding Data
To add data, the INSERT command is used like so:
`INSERT INTO table_name (column names) VALUES (values for each column)`

Here is the example from the book:
```
INSERT INTO SIMPSON_INFO (NAME, GENDER, AGE,
OCCUPATION) VALUES ('Bart Simpson', 'Male', 10,
'Student')
```

Viewing Data
To get data from the database, use the following:
```
SELECT * FROM table_name
```

*Note: * selects all of the columns*

To search for specific data such as a name, we can do the following:
```
SELECT * FROM table_name WHERE name="Some name"
```

With the object that is returned from the SQL command, we can extract the data using:
```
.fetchall()
```

Updating Information
Here is how we updated information in the book:
```
UPDATE SIMPSON_INFO set AGE=41 where NAME='Homer Simpson'
```

Deleting a Row
To delete a row, use the following:
```
DELETE from SIMPSON_INFO where ID=2
```

Delete a table
Here's how to delete a table:
```
DROP TABLE table_name
```

wxPython Quick Reference

Importing wxPython
```
import wx
```

Basic GUI Starter Code
```python
import wx

class Frame(wx.Frame):
    # Added title parameter
    def __init__(self, title):
        # title = title variable
        wx.Frame.__init__(self, None,\
            title=title, size=(300,200))

app = wx.App()
# Pass in the frame title
frame = Frame("Python GUI")
frame.Show()
app.MainLoop()
```

Linking Widgets and Events
The mklbt.Bind()mkrbt function is used. It takes the event parameter and the function to run when the event occurs. Here is an example from the book:

```
button.Bind(wx.EVT_BUTTON, self.exit)
```

Widgets and Events

Here you can find some of the most commonly used widgets and events. To find the full details and events for each widget, I have provided a link to the documentation page.

Widget	Common Event(s)	Documentation
wx.Button	EVT_BUTTON	http://goo.gl/wFaCvZ
wx.ToggleButton	N/A	http://goo.gl/WyHjUm
wx.ComboBox	EVT_COMBOBOX	http://goo.gl/0YP2Qw
wx.CheckBox	EVT_CHECKBOX	http://goo.gl/kPg0zW
wx.ListCtrl	EVT_LIST_ITEM_SELECTED EVT_LIST_ITEM_RIGHT_CLICK	http://goo.gl/EvPSIL
wx.RadioButton	EVT_RADIOBUTTON	http://goo.gl/D9f4CQ
wx.StatusBar	N/A	http://goo.gl/XOoSy5
wx.SpinCtrl	EVT_SPINCTRL	http://goo.gl/XTX6O4
wx.StaticBox	N/A	http://goo.gl/WQDGIS
wx.StaticText	N/A	http://goo.gl/D6ar9c

Special Thanks

Thank you to those who took the time to read Python In A Day 2 in its early stages and helped to create the book in your hands. Without you, Python In A Day 2 wouldn't have been a fraction as good as it turned out.

You know who you are :)

Once again, thank you!

Made in the USA
Lexington, KY
30 September 2014